To

Leah Woods

From

Alice Vandeweele

Date

_11-2-'08_

Daily Inspirations of Love

© 2007 Christian Art Gifts, RSA
          Christian Art Gifts Inc., IL, USA

Designed by Christian Art Gifts

Scripture quotations are taken from the *Holy Bible*, New International
Version®. NIV®. Copyright © 1973, 1978, 1984 by International Bible
Society. Used by permission of Zondervan Publishing House. All rights
reserved.

Printed in China

ISBN 978-1-86920-364-1

08 09 10 11 12 13 14 15 16 17 – 13 12 11 10 9 8 7 6 5 4

dailyinspirations

of
love

Carolyn Larsen

christian
art gifts®

Introduction

What would life be without love? Love is the glue that binds all the other parts of life together. It begins with God's love for you. His love is complete and pure.

Recognizing and accepting His love strengthens all other loves. Returning His love deepens the reservoirs of love itself. Human love that is given and received encourages and connects you with others, giving purpose to life.

The ability to love and be loved is truly a gift. Life without love would be empty and lonely. Thank God for His love today and tell the loved ones in your world how much they mean to you.

Where's the Love?

Change is inevitable. Life is not static. People come and go. Children grow up. Jobs disappear. Health disintegrates. Change happens. Most people do not handle change well.

As these changes happen, your foundations may be shaken. Questions may race through your mind – where is God in all of this? Does He know what's going on? Does He care? Where is His plan? Does He still love me? And the whispered answer to that last question may be, "I don't feel His love."

Believing in God's love must become a non-negotiable principle in your life. You must believe it even when you don't feel it. The "feeling" of God's love may be difficult to find in the hard times when emotions run high and fear and loneliness lurk in your heart.

That's when it is most important to *know* from the words of Scripture and from the character of God that He does, indeed, love you ... forever and always, in good times and hard times. He said it. He showed it. Believe it.

Who shall separate us from the love of Christ? Shall trouble or hardship or persecution or famine or nakedness or danger or sword? No, in all these things we are more than conquerors through Him who loved us. Neither height nor depth, nor anything else in all creation, will be able to separate us from the love of God that is in Christ Jesus our Lord.

Romans 8:35, 37, 39

From everlasting to everlasting the LORD's love is with those who fear Him, and His righteousness with their children's children.

Psalm 103:17

"So do not fear, for I am with you; do not be dismayed, for I am your God. I will strengthen you and help you; I will uphold you with My righteous right hand."

Isaiah 41:10

"I have loved you with an everlasting love; I have drawn you with loving-kindness."

Jeremiah 31:3

How great is the love the Father has lavished on us, that we should be called children of God! And that is what we are!

I John 3:1

This is love: not that we loved God, but that He loved us and sent His Son as an atoning sacrifice for our sins.

I John 4:10

I pray that you, being rooted and established in love, may have power, together with all the saints, to grasp how wide and long and high and deep is the love of Christ, and to know this love that surpasses knowledge – that you may be filled to the measure of all the fullness of God.

Ephesians 3:17-19

God proved His love on the Cross.
When Christ hung, and bled,
and died, it was God saying
to the world, "I love you."
~ Billy Graham

Dear Father, just these words tell me how much You love me. Help me to remember that You are with me, loving me, even when I can't feel that love. I'm never alone or on my own. I want to be able to rest in the knowledge that You love me ... always ... no matter what. In Jesus' loving name I pray.

Amen.

You Want Me to What?

"Love her? You want me to forgive everything and love her? What about the way she treated me – the lies, the disappointments, the pain? Love her? Why should I?"

The pain of betrayal runs deep. Disappointment and hurt lie on your heart like stones. Why should you forgive and forget? It's true that it isn't easy, but there is Someone who constantly does it when the wrong to be forgiven is a lot bigger than what you must forgive. And the love that follows proves that all is forgotten. That's right – Jesus daily models love and forgiveness.

He forgives you, sometimes repeatedly for the same sin. But the necessity of constant forgiveness never interferes with His total and complete love. "Wait," you say, "He's God. Of course He can do that." That's true, but the wonderful thing is that He's willing to help you forgive and forget, too. As you accept His forgiveness and love, it will begin to flow from your heart to others. Forgive. Forget. Love ... it's the only way.

"A new command I give you: Love one another. As I have loved you so you must love one another. By this all men will know that you are My disciples, if you love one another."

John 13:34-35

Now that you have purified yourselves by obeying the truth so that you have sincere love for your brothers, love one another deeply, from the heart.

1 Peter 1:22

"Do not seek revenge or bear a grudge against one of your people, but love your neighbor as yourself. I am the LORD."

Leviticus 19:18

"'Love the Lord your God with all your heart and with all your soul and with all your mind.' This is the first and greatest commandment. And the second is like it: 'Love your neighbor as yourself.'"

Matthew 22:37-39

You are a forgiving God, gracious and compassionate, slow to anger and abounding in love.

Nehemiah 9:17

"My command is this: Love each other as I have loved you. Greater love has no one than this, that he lay down his life for his friends."

John 15:12-13

May the Lord make your love increase and overflow for each other and for everyone else, just as ours does for you.

I Thessalonians 3:12

The LORD is gracious and compassionate, slow to anger and rich in love.

Psalm 145:8

Love is not only something you feel.
It is something you do.
~ David Wilkerson

❧

Dear Father, sometimes this love stuff isn't easy. I find myself wanting to get even instead of loving. Help me to remember that You love me and forgive me, over and over. I want to give that kind of love and forgiveness, too.

I know my friend didn't really intend to hurt me. So, please love through me. Help me forgive, forget and love her just as You love me. In Jesus' name.

Amen.

Amazed!

O God, You are amazing! Since I've met You, my understanding of what love is has grown by a million percent. You have no hidden agenda except to make me a better person. You continually forgive me, guide me, bless me, teach me and ... love me.

All of creation in its beauty and intricacy shows how much pleasure You take in giving me things to look at, marvel on, and enjoy. The most amazing evidence of Your love is Jesus. Sending Your only Son to this planet full of undeserving people with the only purpose of love for those people ... for me ... shows sacrificial, unselfish love.

You adopted me into Your family; You promise me eternity with You; You give guidance and strength in the dailyness of life. I can see where my neediness and disobedience could be a drain on Your love, but You never make me feel that way. Your love is steady, strong and true. It always pulls me in the right direction.

"For God so loved the world that He gave His one and only Son, that whoever believes in Him shall not perish but have eternal life."

John 3:16

God demonstrates His own love for us in this: While we were still sinners, Christ died for us.

Romans 5:8

This is how we know what love is: Jesus Christ laid down His life for us. And we ought to lay down our lives for our brothers.

1 John 3:16

I trust in Your unfailing love; my heart rejoices in Your salvation.

Psalm 13:5

"Even to your old age and gray hairs I am He, I am He who will sustain you. I have made you and I will carry you; I will sustain you and I will rescue you."

Isaiah 46:4

For I am convinced that neither death nor life, neither angels nor demons, neither the present nor the future, nor any powers, neither height nor depth, nor anything else in all creation, will be able to separate us from the love of God that is in Christ Jesus our Lord.

Romans 8:38-39

For the LORD is good and His love endures forever; His faithfulness continues through all generations.

Psalm 100:5

We love because He first loved us.

1 John 4:19

This then is salvation. When we marvel at the beauty of created things and praise their beautiful Creator.
~ *Meister Eckhart*

Dear Father, I am amazed by You. I am humbled, quieted and sometimes stunned that You love me so much. Thank You for guiding and directing me through this life.

Thank You for Your strength and help each and every day. Thank You for hanging in there with me when I'm unlovable and disobedient. Thank You for Your love. I'm so unworthy and yet so very thankful.

Amen.

A Scary Place

This world is a scary place. We humans have perfected the art of hurting others – emotionally and physically.

Does hearing about what's happening around the world – senseless murders, persecutions, hunger, disease – send shivers up and down your spine? If you let yourself really think about it, are you terrified?

You need an anchor ... something to hold on to ... something to stabilize your heart when it goes into spasms of terror. If you've looked for that anchor in friends, a career or success, you probably didn't find it.

Perhaps you looked for it in the love of your family but it wasn't there either. Even the best things in life aren't strong enough to protect you from the dangers of this world.

Where can you find the true anchor that can hold you steady? In God. Only in God. His love protects you from whatever this life brings. His love surrounds you; goes before you, guards you on both sides and brings up the rear. His love is all you need.

Even though I walk through the valley of the shadow of death, I will fear no evil, for You are with me; Your rod and Your staff, they comfort me.

Psalm 23:4

Be strong and take heart, all you who hope in the LORD.

Psalm 31:24

For God did not give us a spirit of timidity, but a spirit of power, of love and of self-discipline.

2 Timothy 1:7

There is no fear in love. But perfect love drives out fear, because fear has to do with punishment. The one who fears is not made perfect in love.

1 John 4:18

Because of the LORD's great love we are not consumed, for His compassions never fail. They are new every morning; great is Your faithfulness.

Lamentations 3:22

Greater love has no one than this, that he lay down his life for his friends.

John 15:13

I will sing of the LORD's great love forever; with my mouth I will make Your faithfulness known through all generations.

Psalm 89:1

We rejoice in the hope of the glory of God. Not only so, but we also rejoice in our sufferings, because we know that suffering produces perseverance; perseverance, character; and character, hope. And hope does not disappoint us, because God has poured out His love into our hearts by the Holy Spirit, whom He has given us.

Romans 5:2-5

All I have seen teaches me to trust
the Creator for all I have not seen.
~ Ralph Waldo Emerson

*Dear Father, I long to trust Your love more
every day. I believe that perfect love casts
away our fears. So the fear in my heart has
to leave when I begin to trust Your love. Help
me to understand, Father. Help me to grasp
what it means that You love me.*

Amen.

Loving My Friends

Friends are awesome. A friend's love is like God's love ... with skin. With friends you can get silly and laugh so hard your stomach hurts. But when life hits hard, friends will cry with you or just stick around until things are better. It's wonderful to share in each other's lives – the good times and the sad times.

Really close friends can point out when you're being unfair or unreasonable. You'll listen because you know they love you and want to help. They care about your happiness and know that your attitudes are often what keep you down. Friendship is reciprocal so you do the same things for them.

Friends see that your heart is mostly kind, but sometimes has rough edges. They take the good with the bad and just love you through it ... and you love them right back.

The love between friends is an example of God's love. Friends are a gift from God. They are just one more way He shows His love to you.

A friend loves at all times, and a brother is born for adversity.

Proverbs 17:17

The entire law is summed up in a single command: "Love your neighbor as yourself."

Galatians 5:14

Love does no harm to its neighbor. Therefore love is the fulfillment of the law.

Romans 13:10

Now about brotherly love we do not need to write to you, for you yourselves have been taught by God to love each other.

1 Thessalonians 4:9

Perfume and incense bring joy to the heart, and the pleasantness of one's friend springs from his earnest counsel.

Proverbs 27:9

Dear friends, let us love one another for love comes from God. Everyone who loves has been born of God and knows God.

I John 4:7

Dear children, let us not love with words or tongue but with actions and in truth.

I John 3:18

Your love, O LORD, reaches to the heavens, Your faithfulness to the skies.

Psalm 36:5

The LORD your God is with you, He is mighty to save. He will take great delight in you, He will quiet you with His love, He will rejoice over you with singing.

Zephaniah 3:17

Friendship is the most constant,
the most enduring,
the most basic part of love.
                              ~ Ed Cunningham

Dear Father, thank You for my friends. I appreciate them so much. Thank You for loving me through them, teaching me through them, and encouraging me through them. Help me to be a good friend to each of them.

                              Amen.

Patient Love

Of course you love your friends and family. But, if you were completely honest, you would have to admit that sometimes they really annoy you. Things would be so much easier if they did things the way you want, made the choices you believe are right, just let you run their lives ... right?

Okay, there may be some control issues there. But even for the best of us, there are times when patience is a virtue that isn't at the top of our character traits. The conflict is that Scripture tells us that real love is patient. It doesn't have control issues, it puts up with others' faults and while God doesn't insist that we like other people's actions or choices, we must still love them.

After all, Christ consistently models patient love for us. From a human viewpoint we test His love with our constant disobedience and focus on self, but He just keeps on loving ... patiently loving.

Love is patient, love is kind. It does not envy, it does not boast, it is not proud.

I Corinthians 13:4

Whoever loves his brother lives in the light, and there is nothing in him to make him stumble. But whoever hates his brother is in the darkness; he does not know where he is going, because the darkness has blinded him.

I John 2:10-11

No one has ever seen God; but if we love one another, God lives in us and His love is made complete in us.

I John 4:11

A man's wisdom gives him patience; it is to his glory to overlook an offense.

Proverbs 19:12

The Lord is slow to anger, abounding in love and forgiving sin and rebellion.

Numbers 14:18

Know therefore that the Lord your God is God; He is the faithful God, keeping His covenant of love to a thousand generations of those who love Him and keep His commands.

Deuteronomy 7:9

Bear with each other and forgive whatever grievances you may have against one another. Forgive as the Lord forgave you. And over all these virtues put on love, which binds them all together in perfect unity.

Colossians 3:13-14

Be completely humble and gentle; be patient, bearing with one another in love.

Ephesians 4:2

*A handful of patience is worth
more than a bushel of brains.*

~ Dutch Proverb

❧

*Dear Father, patience doesn't seem to come
naturally to me. I need some help from You
to be more patient and forgiving with those
around me. Help me to love my family and
friends as You love me.*

Amen.

Tough Love

Sometimes love hurts. It's hard when a loved one continually makes bad choices that impact her life and the lives of those around her. The natural response is to try to help get her life back on track. It's painful to stand by and watch someone self-destruct.

When you try to help, over and over, but never see any progress – then it's time to make a decision. It may seem like an oxymoron but sometimes the way to show love to someone is to just stop trying. Tough love.

Of course, even if you must physically walk away from a loved one, your heart never stops loving. The only thing you can do then is trust her to God.

Remember that He made her. She is His creation. He knows the choices she's making and can see the future implications.

Remember more than anything else that He loves her, even more than you do.

Give thanks to the Lord, for He is good; His love endures forever.

I Chronicles 16:34

Many waters cannot quench love; rivers cannot wash it away.

Song of Songs 8:7

Because of His great love for us, God, who is rich in mercy, made us alive with Christ even when we were dead in transgressions – it is by grace you have been saved.

Ephesians 2:4-5

May our Lord Jesus Christ Himself and God our Father, who loved us and by His grace gave us eternal encouragement and good hope, encourage your hearts and strengthen you in every good deed and word.

2 Thessalonians 2:16-17

"As a mother comforts her child, so will I comfort you."

Isaiah 66:13

I love the LORD, for He heard my voice; He heard my cry for mercy. Because He turned His ear to me, I will call on Him as long as I live.

Psalm 116:1-2

"As the Father has loved Me, so have I loved you."

John 15:9

Give thanks to the LORD, for He is good; His love endures forever.

Psalm 107:1

Praise the LORD, O my soul, and forget not all His benefits – who forgives all your sins and heals all your diseases, who redeems your life from the pit and crowns you with love and compassion.

Psalm 103:2-4

No matter how steep the mountain,
the Lord is going to climb it with you.
~ Helen Steiner Rice

❧

Dear Father, forgive me, but I tend to think that I have to "fix" my loved ones instead of trusting them to You. Help me remember that You know what's happening and You can see down the road, too.

More than anything, help me remember that You love my loved ones even more than I do.

Amen.

In the Waiting Room

What is taking God so long? You've prayed and prayed for His guidance and direction to be clear. But when you look out at the options for your future, everything is still a foggy mess.

Does it seem as if He keeps you in the "waiting room" when you seek His will? As time drags on and confusion grows, do you find yourself beginning to question if He's paying attention ... if you matter to Him ... if He really loves you?

There's no doubt about it, waiting is hard! However, it's important to remember that it is in the waiting room where your faith will grow the most. In the waiting room you learn that you can depend on God. You discover that you must be still to hear His voice.

More than anything else, you'll learn that God loves you too much to just tell you what to do, He wants to help you learn to trust Him and love Him more and more.

In Your unfailing love You will lead the people You have redeemed. In Your strength You will guide them to Your holy dwelling.

Exodus 15:13

You prepare a table before me in the presence of my enemies. You anoint my head with oil; my cup overflows. Surely goodness and love will follow me all the days of my life, and I will dwell in the house of the Lord forever.

Psalm 23:5-6

Blessed is the man who perseveres under trial, because when he has stood the test, he will receive the crown of life that God has promised to those who love Him.

James 1:12

May the Lord direct your hearts into God's love and Christ's perseverance.

2 Thessalonians 3:5

Show me Your ways, O Lord, teach me Your paths; guide me in Your truth and teach me, for You are God my Savior, and my hope is in You all day long.

Psalm 25:4-5

For He chose us in Him before the creation of the world to be holy and blameless in His sight. In love He predestined us to be adopted as His sons through Jesus Christ, in accordance with His pleasure and will – to the praise of His glorious grace, which He has freely given us in the One He loves.

Ephesians 1:4-6

He guides the humble in what is right and teaches them His way. All the ways of the Lord are loving and faithful for those who keep the demands of His covenant.

Psalm 25:9-10

*What we believe about God is
the most important thing about us.*
~ A.W. Tozer

*Dear Father, forgive me for wanting to take
the easy way out. I do want my faith to grow.
I want to trust You more and love You more
deeply. I guess I have to spend time in the
waiting room before that can happen.*

*Help me to remember that the time I
spend there is evidence of how much You love
me and want me to grow.*

Amen.

A Mother's Love

A mother stands in the doorway of a darkened room watching her young child sleep. Her heart is once again overwhelmed with love for this little one. Who knew she was capable of so much love? From the instant this child entered her life, the instinct to love, protect, provide for, bring joy to, teach and nurture, burst into her heart. She would do anything for this child.

Whether you become a mother by birth or by choice, the opportunity to raise a child is a blessing. It's not always easy to be a mom. Sometimes you may feel as if you're wearing your heart on the outside and every single thing that hurts or threatens your child tears at your own heart.

On the other hand, every hug or smile, every "You're the best mommy in the world" swells your heart with more and more love. There's no doubt about it, children are a gift from God and every day as a mom is a lesson in love.

Sons are a heritage from the Lord, children a reward from Him.

Psalm 127:3

Thanks be to God for His indescribable gift.

2 Corinthians 9:15

Every good and perfect gift is from above, coming
down from the Father of the heavenly lights, who
does not change like shifting shadows. He chose
to give us birth through the word of truth, that we
might be a kind of firstfruits of all He created.

James 1:17-18

Return to the Lord your God, for He is gracious
and compassionate, slow to anger and abounding
in love.

Joel 2:13

Let love and faithfulness never leave you; bind
them around your neck, write them on the tablet
of your heart.

Proverbs 3:3

You show that you are a letter from Christ, the result of our ministry, written not with ink but with the Spirit of the living God, not on tablets of stone but on tablets of human hearts.

2 Corinthians 3:3

While He was still speaking, a bright cloud enveloped them, and a voice from the cloud said, "This is My Son, whom I love; with Him I am well pleased. Listen to Him!"

Matthew 17:5

*Making the decision to have
a child is momentous. It is to decide
forever to have your heart go
walking around outside your body.*
~ Elizabeth Stone

❧

*Dear Father, I love being a mom. Thank You
for my children. Help me to model Your love
to them and teach them about You by the
way I live my life in front of them.*

Amen.

Love Is Kind

"I'm tired. I'm frustrated and the last thing in the world that I want to do is be nice. I want to yell at people to get out of my way. I want to insist on being served and on everyone doing things the way I want. Do you hear me? I don't feel like being kind!"

Sound familiar? Well, at least it's honest. The truth is that everyone feels like this sometimes. Most people don't actually verbalize it, but that doesn't mean it's not bouncing around in the mind and heart of potentially any person you meet during the day.

Being kind when you don't feel like it is a choice. It's an opportunity to put actions to words of love. But on a bad day even the kindest person is going to need extra help to actually be kind to others.

Ask God for that help. After all, He's the author of love and He will fill you with all the kindness you need to get through the day.

Make sure that nobody pays back wrong for wrong, but always try to be kind to each other and to everyone else.

I Thessalonians 5:15

Love is kind.

I Corinthians 13:4

Be kind and compassionate to one another, forgiving each other, just as in Christ God forgave you.

Ephesians 4:32

The LORD loves righteousness and justice; the earth is full of His unfailing love.

Psalm 33:5

One thing God has spoken, two things have I heard: that You, O God, are strong, and that You, O LORD, are loving. Surely You will reward each person according to what he has done.

Psalm 62:11-12

Whoever would love life and see good days must keep his tongue from evil and his lips from deceitful speech.

1 Peter 3:10

[Love] always protects, always trusts, always hopes, always perseveres.

1 Corinthians 13:7

An anxious heart weighs a man down, but a kind word cheers him up.

Proverbs 12:25

He who despises his neighbor sins, but blessed is he who is kind to the needy.

Proverbs 14:21

The Lord's servant must not quarrel; instead, he must be kind to everyone, able to teach, not resentful.

2 Timothy 2:24

*We are all called upon
to do small things with great love.*

~ *Mother Teresa*

❧

*Dear Father, I need Your help to be loving
when I don't feel like it. I know that the times
when I'm tired and grouchy are opportuni-
ties to let Your love flow through me. That's
when others will be able to see that You control my life. Please help me.*

Amen.

Strong Love

Have you stopped lately and thought about God's love for you? Really thought about it? It's so easy to take God's many gifts for granted, especially as life gets busier and busier. You may begin to simply expect the blessings of God to be there every day. Take some time right now to recognize the ways God shows His love to you.

Start with the gift of Jesus which shows His sacrificial love for you. Then think about the beautiful world He created for you to live in with majestic mountains, powerful oceans, gentle meadows and peaceful fields. Think about the precious people He has placed in your life. Think about the privilege of prayer – being able to talk to God anytime you want.

His Word is another evidence of His love because it lets you know Him better and learn His principles for living. God supplies strength, power and wisdom to guide you through this life. His thoughts are always on you. He loves you.

Sing to the LORD, for He has done glorious things; let this be known to all the world.

Isaiah 12:5

The LORD is good, a refuge in times of trouble. He cares for those who trust in Him.

Nahum 1:7

By day the LORD directs His love, at night His song is with me – a prayer to the God of my life.

Psalm 42:8

"I in them and You in Me. May they be brought to complete unity to let the world know that You sent Me and have loved them even as You have loved Me."

John 17:23

He has rescued us from the dominion of darkness and brought us into the kingdom of the Son He loves, in whom we have redemption, the forgiveness of sins.

Colossians 1:13

Hope does not disappoint us, because God has poured out His love into our hearts by the Holy Spirit, whom He has given us.

Romans 5:5

This is how God showed His love among us: He sent His one and only Son into the world that we might live through Him.

I John 4:9

Because Your love is better than life, my lips will glorify You.

Psalm 63:3

I will tell of the kindnesses of the LORD, the deeds for which He is to be praised, according to all the LORD has done for us – yes, the many good things He has done for the house of Israel, according to His compassion and many kindnesses.

Isaiah 63:7

Our God is omnipotent.
There can be no limit, boundary,
or edge to His ability and power.
~ Paris Reidhead

❧

Dear Father, the reality of Your love just blows me away. I'm amazed by its power, generosity and consistence. Thank You for loving me so completely.

Amen.

God's Love

Do you recognize these thoughts: "Arrghh! I keep making the same mistakes over and over. I lose my temper at the same things and think the same critical thoughts. Why can't I learn to stop committing the same sins? How can God keep on loving me when I continually disappoint Him? Sin seems to be my middle name!"

When you consider your constant, if unintentional, disobedience, it is a mystery that God doesn't give up on you, isn't it? But stop and think about God's character which is shown in the Old Testament by how He related to His people. They failed and disobeyed God over and over and He kept right on loving them.

Scripture itself explains it best, "God is love," is what we read in 1 John. His character is love; true love. God cannot act contrary to His character. That's the simple answer to why God forgives your shortcomings and sins and just keeps on loving you.

The LORD our God is merciful and forgiving, even though we have rebelled against Him.

Daniel 9:9

For as high as the heavens are above the earth, so great is His love for those who fear Him; as far as the east is from the west, so far has He removed our transgressions from us.

Psalm 103:11-12

I have been crucified with Christ and I no longer live, but Christ lives in me. The life I live in the body, I live by faith in the Son of God, who loved me and gave Himself for me.

Galatians 2:20

Keep yourselves in God's love as you wait for the mercy of our Lord Jesus Christ to bring you to eternal life.

Jude 21

If anyone obeys His word, God's love is truly made complete in him.

1 John 2:5

To Him who loves us and has freed us from our sins by His blood, and has made us to be a kingdom and priests to serve His God and Father – to Him be glory and power for ever and ever!

Revelation 1:5-6

"Therefore, I tell you, her many sins have been forgiven – for she loved much. But he who has been forgiven little loves little."

Luke 7:47

For Christ's love compels us, because we are convinced that one died for all, and therefore all died.

2 Corinthians 5:14

God is even kinder than you think.
~ St. Theresa

Dear Father, I'm so humbled by Your loving forgiveness. Thank You for giving me chance after chance to grow and mature. I'm learning ... slowly ... because of Your forgiving love that never gives up on me.

Amen.

Risky Love

It's easiest to love people who are like you, right? Those who have similar beliefs and standards and are in the same economic place are most comfortable for you to love. Perhaps you even gravitate to those who have similar interests or hobbies. It's comfortable to be around people who are like you.

There's nothing wrong with loving your friends. But that's the easy love. How do you relate to those who aren't Christians or are antagonistic to anything spiritual?

Those who are on a much lower or higher economic standard? Those from a political party whose views make you so angry you could ... well, you know. How about anyone who disagrees with you about war, abortion or has a different stand on gay rights? Are we getting too close to home?

It's hard to love people who are really different from you. In fact, it may be nearly impossible without God loving through you. He's willing to do that because He commands you to love others ... especially those who are different.

"This is My command: Love each other."

John 15:17

This is the message you heard from the beginning: We should love one another.

1 John 3:11

Direct my footsteps according to Your word; let no sin rule over me.

Psalm 119:133

A gentle answer turns away wrath, but a harsh word stirs up anger.

Proverbs 15:1

Jesus replied, "'Do not murder, do not commit adultery, do not steal, do not give false testimony, honor your father and mother,' and 'love your neighbor as yourself.'"

Matthew 19:18-19

Above all, love each other deeply, because love covers over a multitude of sins.

1 Peter 4:8

Love must be sincere. Hate what is evil; cling to what is good. Be devoted to one another in brotherly love. Honor one another above yourselves.

Romans 12:9-10

The goal of this command is love, which comes from a pure heart and a good conscience and a sincere faith.

1 Timothy 1:5

We know that we have passed from death to life, because we love our brothers. Anyone who does not love remains in death.

1 John 3:14

Do not forget to entertain strangers, for by so doing some people have entertained angels without knowing it.

Hebrews 13:2

Our Lord does not care so much for the importance of our works, as for the love with which they are done.

~ Anonymous

Dear Father, some people are just so hard to love. It's easier to justify my dislike or to just stay away from them. But, what's easy isn't always what's right. Please open my heart and love these people through me. Let them see You through my love.

Amen.

Sacrificial Love

Love is a word that is liberally tossed around today. "I love this TV show." "Don't you just love that song?" "I LOVE chocolate!"

We love everything from hairstyles to movie stars. But do we really *love* those things? Would our lives be any different if those things or movie stars or singers weren't part of them? Probably not. Oh sure, perhaps we would miss some of the things (chocolate, for example). But we'd certainly survive.

Have we cheapened the meaning of love by spreading it so thin? Love that costs something is love at a deeper level. The depth of love that God showed when Jesus came to live and die on this little planet is love at its greatest.

His love is pure and deep. It is sacrificial love and yes, our lives would be vastly different without it. God's love wraps us in a security blanket because the Creator of the universe, the great I AM loves us so much that He gave His only Son. That's real love.

For to us a Child is born, to us a Son is given, and the government will be on His shoulders. And He will be called Wonderful Counselor, Mighty God, Everlasting Father, Prince of Peace.

Isaiah 9:6

"For God did not send His Son into the world to condemn the world, but to save the world through Him."

John 3:17

"Greater love has no one than this, that he lay down his life for his friends."

John 15:13

He will cover you with His feathers, and under His wings you will find refuge; His faithfulness will be your shield and rampart.

Psalm 91:4

The Lord lives! Praise be to my Rock! Exalted be God, the Rock, my Savior!

2 Samuel 22:47

The sacrifices of God are a broken spirit; a broken and contrite heart, O God, You will not despise.

Psalm 51:17

And now these three remain: faith, hope and love. But the greatest of these is love.

I Corinthians 13:13

We love because He first loved us.

I John 4:19

Be imitators of God, therefore, as dearly loved children and live a life of love, just as Christ loved us and gave Himself up for us as a fragrant offering and sacrifice to God.

Ephesians 5:1-2

*Who among the sons of men
ever loved God with a thousandth
part of the love which God
has manifested to us?*

~ *Anonymous*

❧

*Dear Father, I guess I do throw the "love" word
around pretty freely. I ask You now to help
me to be still and think about Your love for
me and what that love cost You. Help me to
understand and to be truly, fully grateful.*

Amen.

Christmastime

Christmas – when we're filled with love for everyone – unless of course, you're in a crowded toy store grabbing for the last available hot toy of the season.

At Christmas our hearts are filled with love for family and friends. We diligently search for just the right gifts to show them how much we care. Even the world thinks about God more at Christmastime and warmly appreciates the gift of the little baby whose birth we're celebrating.

Wouldn't it be wonderful if we could bottle that Christmas love and enjoy it all year long? The world would be a kinder place. We'd be more generous with those in need; making an effort to see that everyone has food and a warm place to sleep; that children have toys and laughter in their lives.

We'd be more forgiving of others' shortcomings. As you read these words do you kind of wonder if this behavior was what God had in mind when He wrote, "Love one another?" You're probably right.

For this very reason, make every effort to add to your faith goodness; and to goodness, knowledge; and to knowledge, self-control; and to self-control, perseverance; and to perseverance, godliness; and to godliness, brotherly kindness; and to brotherly kindness, love.

2 Peter 1:5-7

"By this all men will know that you are My disciples, if you love one another."

John 13:35

Everyone who believes that Jesus is the Christ is born of God, and everyone who loves the Father loves His Child as well.

1 John 5:1

Let us consider how we may spur one another on toward love and good deeds.

Hebrews 10:24

The LORD is my strength and my song; He has become my salvation. He is my God, and I will praise Him, my father's God, and I will exalt Him.

Exodus 15:2

Therefore the LORD Himself will give you a sign: The virgin will be with child and will give birth to a son, and will call Him Immanuel.

Isaiah 7:14

My purpose is that they may be encouraged in heart and united in love, so that they may have the full riches of complete understanding, in order that they may know the mystery of God, namely, Christ, in whom are hidden all the treasures of wisdom and knowledge.

Colossians 2:2-3

If you, then, though you are evil, know how to give good gifts to your children, how much more will your Father in heaven give good gifts to those who ask Him!

Matthew 7:11

The coming of Christ by way of a Bethlehem manger seems strange and stunning. But when we take Him out of the manger and invite Him into our hearts, then the meaning unfolds and the strangeness vanishes.

~ C. Neil Strait

❧

Dear Father, I want to get out of my comfort zone and experience "Christmas love" all year long. Fill me with love for those whose needs make me uncomfortable; those to whom I don't know what to say. Show me how to give action to that love, in Your name.

Amen.

Disciplinary Love

Children would have you think that love means being able to: eat junk food before dinner, stay up late, watch any TV show or movie they want, disobey with no consequences, or only do their homework when they feel like it. In other words, all freedom, all the time.

Parents, of course, know that isn't true. Love involves discipline as you help your children learn to become responsible people and contributing members of society. Disciplinary love is difficult but necessary.

The same is true of God's love for His children. He doesn't allow us to run around all willy-nilly, doing whatever we want, obeying when we feel like it or being kind and loving just when it's convenient.

The commands given in the Bible must be obeyed and disobedience has consequences. He doesn't punish us out of meanness or anger, but because of love.

God wants us to be continually growing into more mature believers. Discipline helps that happen. Discipline is given because of love.

The LORD disciplines those He loves, as a father the son he delights in.

Proverbs 3:12

You have forgotten that word of encouragement that addresses you as sons: "My son, do not make light of the Lord's discipline, and do not lose heart when He rebukes you, because the Lord disciplines those He loves, and He punishes everyone He accepts as a son."

Hebrews 12:5-6

Blessed is the man You discipline, O LORD, the man You teach from Your law.

Psalm 94:12

How great is the love the Father has lavished on us, that we should be called children of God!

1 John 3:1

Though your sins are like scarlet, they shall be as white as snow; though they are red as crimson, they shall be like wool.

Isaiah 1:18

God is love. Whoever lives in love lives in God, and God in him. In this way, love is made complete among us so that we will have confidence on the day of judgment, because in this world we are like Him.

I John 4:16-17

The LORD is my shepherd, I shall not be in want. He makes me lie down in green pastures, He leads me beside quiet waters, He restores my soul. He guides me in paths of righteousness for His name's sake.

Psalm 23:1-3

Jesus spoke of Christianity as
a banquet, but never as a picnic.
                    ~ Anonymous

❧

*Dear Father, discipline hurts. I don't like it.
However, I appreciate what it does in my
heart. I appreciate that You want my faith
to grow and mature.*

*Help me to learn from discipline and not
continue making the same mistakes. Teach
me. Grow me into the woman You desire for
me to be.*

Amen.

Receiving Love

Some people are servants who enjoy doing things for others, even going out of their way to help others in any way they can. Their own needs are put aside as they serve others. They could be called sacrificial servants.

There's certainly nothing wrong with that. Serving others is a wonderful way to show love to other people. However, these sacrificial servants sometimes have difficulty accepting the same kind of actions from others. It makes them uncomfortable to accept assistance or help. That's unfortunate and even wrong. There should be no pride taken in refusing to allow others to serve.

Accepting the loving actions of someone else is important because it allows him or her to serve. There is a domino effect to serving. When you are served in love, then you want to pay it forward and serve someone else in love. The giver and the receiver are then connected.

Allowing others to serve is a gift to them because it allows them to love in the way God instructed ... serving others.

"If anyone gives even a cup of cold water to one of these little ones because he is My disciple, I tell you the truth, he will certainly not lose his reward."

Matthew 10:42

He who oppresses the poor shows contempt for their Maker, but whoever is kind to the needy honors God.

Proverbs 14:31

God is not unjust; He will not forget your work and the love you have shown Him as you have helped His people and continue to help them.

Hebrews 6:10

Submit yourselves, then, to God. Resist the devil, and he will flee from you. Come near to God and He will come near to you. Humble yourselves before the Lord, and He will lift you up.

James 4:7-8, 10

This is my prayer: that your love may abound more and more in knowledge and depth of insight, so that you may be able to discern what is best and may be pure and blameless until the day of Christ, filled with the fruit of righteousness that comes through Jesus Christ – to the glory and praise of God.

Philippians 1:9-11

Now about brotherly love we do not need to write to you, for you yourselves have been taught by God to love each other.

1 Thessalonians 4:9

I am not writing you a new command but one we have had from the beginning. I ask that we love one another.

2 John 5

"A new command I give you: Love one another. As I have loved you, so you must love one another."

John 13:34

To love and be loved is to feel
the sun from both sides.

~ David Viscott

Dear Father, sometimes I have trouble allowing other people to help me. It's hard to be that vulnerable. Thank You for the reminder that accepting their love and service is a gift to them and that it actually assists them in obeying You.

Amen.

Love in Action

Loving others is a marking point of the Christian life and we hear a lot about it. But what does love look like in everyday life? It's easy to say the words, but putting action behind those words is sometimes difficult. Showing love means giving of your time, energy and even money.

When someone has lost a loved one and she's so lonely she can't bear it, what good is it to say, "Remember, I love you!" Show love by taking her out to dinner and listening as she talks through her pain. You don't need the answers – all she needs is to know someone cares.

Another friend might be overwhelmed with the work of a new baby and toddlers to care for. Showing love would be taking a dinner in, taking the toddlers out, or staying with all the children while she gets away for a couple of hours.

Loving others is more than just saying loving words. It's important to put feet and hands to it to give love life.

Comfort, comfort My people, says your God.

Isaiah 40:1

If I speak in the tongues of men and of angels, but have not love, I am only a resounding gong or a clanging cymbal.

I Corinthians 13:1

Then the righteous will answer Him, "Lord, when did we see You hungry and feed You, or thirsty and give You something to drink? When did we see You a stranger and invite You in, or needing clothes and clothe You? When did we see You sick or in prison and go to visit You?" Then the King will reply, "I tell you the truth, whatever you did for one of the least of these brothers of Mine, you did for Me."

Matthew 25:37-40

"Now that I, your Lord and Teacher, have washed your feet, you also should wash one another's feet."

John 13:14

Therefore encourage one another and build each other up, just as in fact you are doing.

I Thessalonians 5:11

Now you are the body of Christ, and each one of you is a part of it.

I Corinthians 12:27

Clothe yourselves with humility toward one another, because God opposes the proud but gives grace to the humble.

I Peter 5:5

Do not withhold good from those who deserve it, when it is in your power to act. Do not say to your neighbor, "Come back later; I'll give it tomorrow" – when you have it with you.

Proverbs 3:27-28

You can give without loving,
but you cannot love without giving.
~ Amy Carmichael

Dear Father, it's easy to say that I love others, then just walk away from people with needs or problems. But my love only shows when I put action to it. Please keep reminding me to take the time, make the effort and find a way to put love into action.

Amen.

Love Letters

A special guy, romantic dinners, moonlight walks, carriage rides ... ahh, falling in love. It's wonderful. Even more special is when he sends a card or note with his loving thoughts written inside. You read it often, imagining his voice and seeing the love in his eyes. Treasured love letters are bundled together and tied with ribbon or kept in a special box. They are a record of your growing love for one another.

God has sent you love letters, too. His Word, the Bible, is filled with descriptions of His love for you. It tells of His sacrifices for you, His plans for you, His hopes for you. It describes what He has already done for you and His other loved ones.

The words of Scripture affirm His unfailing, eternal commitment to you. He loves you and He wants you to know that. Read His Word as if it were a love letter. You'll be overwhelmed with the extravagance of His love for you.

How sweet are Your words to my taste, sweeter than honey to my mouth.

Psalm 119:103

"Whoever has My commands and obeys them, he is the one who loves Me."

John 14:21

For these commands are a lamp, this teaching is a light, and the corrections of discipline are the way to life.

Proverbs 6:23

I have hidden Your word in my heart that I might not sin against You.

Psalm 119:11

All Scripture is God-breathed and is useful for teaching, rebuking, correcting and training in righteousness, so that the man of God may be thoroughly equipped for every good work.

2 Timothy 3:16

Do not let this Book of the Law depart from your mouth; meditate on it day and night, so that you may be careful to do everything written in it. Then you will be prosperous and successful.

Joshua 1:8

These commandments that I give you today are to be upon your hearts. Impress them on your children. Talk about them when you sit at home and when you walk along the road, when you lie down and when you get up.

Deuteronomy 6:6-7

For the word of God is living and active. Sharper than any double-edged sword, it penetrates even to dividing soul and spirit, joints and marrow; it judges the thoughts and attitudes of the heart.

Hebrews 4:12

When you read God's Word, you must
constantly be saying to yourself,
"It is talking to me and about me."

~ Sören Kierkegaard

Dear Father, I'm so thankful for Your Word.
The more I read it, the more I love it. Thank
You for teaching me and challenging me
through it. Thank You for caring enough to
give me the Bible so that I can know You better.

Amen.

Loving God

Scripture tells us in many places that loving God means obeying Him. For example, John 14:21 says, "Whoever has My commands and obeys them, he is the one who loves Me."

To say that you love Him but deliberately disobey Him makes your words of love a lie. It's relatively easy to hide disobedience from others – some sins are sins of the heart which no one but you (and God) would know about. You can "do" all the right things – go to church, read your Bible and pray, but if your heart is filled with rebellion that plays out in some secret sin – then you're not obeying.

"Love the Lord your God with all your heart and with all your soul and with all your mind. This is the first and greatest commandment" (Matt. 22:37-38).

Blending the words of John 14:21 and Matthew 22:37-38 confirms that it is impossible to love God without obeying Him. Don't bother with the rest of it if you're not willing to obey.

Love the LORD your God with all your heart and with all your soul and with all your strength.

Deuteronomy 6:5

"I will walk among you and be your God, and you will be My people."

Leviticus 26:12

Be very careful to keep the commandment and the law that Moses the servant of the LORD gave you: to love the LORD your God, to walk in all His ways, to obey His commands, to hold fast to Him and to serve Him with all your heart and all your soul.

Joshua 22:5

I love the LORD, for He heard my voice; He heard my cry for mercy.

Psalm 116:1

All the ways of the Lord are loving and faithful for those who keep the demands of His covenant.

Psalm 25:10

"The most important [commandment]," answered Jesus, "is this: Hear, O Israel, the Lord our God, the Lord is one. Love the Lord your God with all your heart and with all your soul and with all your mind and with all your strength."

Mark 12:29-30

God is not unjust; He will not forget your work and the love you have shown Him as you have helped His people and continue to help them.

Hebrews 6:10

The knowledge of Christ's love for us should cause us to love Him in such a way that it is demonstrated in our attitude, conduct and commitment to serve God. Spiritual maturity is marked by spiritual knowledge being put into action.

~ Edward Bedore

ॐ

Dear Father, I love You. I honestly do. It's just that the obeying thing is so hard sometimes. I feel like I continually disobey in the same places over and over. Father, help me to learn. Help me to be strong. Help me to love You more and more by obeying more and more.

Amen.

Loving Yourself

"If only I could sing the way she does." "Why aren't I prettier?", "I should be thinner ... smarter ... more successful ... " Do you sometimes compare yourself to others and feel that you come up short? It's a temptation to long for the gifts or talents that other people have.

Some people get so caught up in this comparison that they have difficulty loving themselves. Then they find it hard to believe that anyone else could love them either.

Fight this downward spiral by remembering that God didn't make any second-class people. He didn't create an A-list, then use the left-over parts to make a lesser creation. God creates each person with abilities, gifts, and a heart to give in love. Of course every person is different, some have more "out in front" gifts than others. But all are necessary to make the family of God healthy.

No one is more important than another. God loves each of His children – believe it and love yourself, too.

God created man in His own image, in the image of God He created him; male and female He created them.

Genesis 1:27

For You created my inmost being; You knit me together in my mother's womb. I praise You because I am fearfully and wonderfully made; Your works are wonderful, I know that full well.

Psalm 139:13-14

My frame was not hidden from You when I was made in the secret place. When I was woven together in the depths of the earth, Your eyes saw my unformed body. All the days ordained for me were written in Your book before one of them came to be.

Psalm 139:15-16

"Are not two sparrows sold for a penny? Yet not one of them will fall to the ground apart from the will of your Father. And even the very hairs of your head are all numbered. So don't be afraid; you are worth more than many sparrows."

Matthew 10:29-31

We have different gifts, according to the grace given us.

Romans 12:6

The body is a unit, though it is made up of many parts; and though all its parts are many, they form one body. Now you are the body of Christ, and each one of you is a part of it.

1 Corinthians 12:12, 27

God loves each of us as if
there were only one of us.

~ *St. Augustine*

❧

Dear Father, I've heard it said that "God didn't make no junk." I know that means that I'm supposed to love myself. But, it's hard, because, after all, I know me. I know my inner thoughts and I know my failures.

Please help me to concentrate my thoughts on the fact that You love me. Help me to know the gifts and abilities You've given me. Help me to love myself simply because You love me.

Amen.

Daily Love

There is an old joke where a lonely wife longs to hear her husband say, "I love you." His response is, "I told you once that I love you. If I change my mind, I'll let you know." We smile at this, but only on the outside because even if you know in your heart that someone loves you it's nice to hear the words.

God never makes a statement like that. His love pursues you. The psalmist says that God's love follows him all the days of his life (Ps. 23:6). Think about the ways His love is shown; from something as magnificent, but daily, as the sun coming up every day or the earth staying in it's place in the universe to the precious hug of a child, beauty of a flower or warmth of family.

Even more incredible are His answers to prayer, the guidance and discernment He gives and His strength within you during difficult times. He loves you and when you look for it, you'll hear Him say so every day.

Who shall separate us from the love of Christ? Shall trouble or hardship or persecution or famine or nakedness or danger or sword? No, in all these things we are more than conquerors through Him who loved us.

Romans 8:35, 37

He was pierced for our transgressions, He was crushed for our iniquities; the punishment that brought us peace was upon Him, and by His wounds we are healed.

Isaiah 53:5

The eternal God is your refuge, and underneath are the everlasting arms.

Deuteronomy 33:27

I love You, O Lord, my strength. The Lord is my rock, my fortress and my deliverer; my God is my rock, in whom I take refuge. He is my shield and the horn of my salvation, my stronghold.

Psalm 18:1-2

The Lord is compassionate and gracious, slow to anger, abounding in love. For as high as the heavens are above the earth, so great is His love for those who fear Him.

Psalm 103:8, 11

"For God so loved the world that He gave His one and only Son, that whoever believes in Him shall not perish but have eternal life."

John 3:16

Because of the Lord's great love we are not consumed, for His compassions never fail. They are new every morning; great is Your faithfulness.

Lamentations 3:22-23

How precious to me are Your thoughts, O God! How vast is the sum of them!

Psalm 139:17

Above all else, know this:
Be prepared at all times for the gifts
of God and be ready always
for new ones. For God is
a thousand times more ready
to give than we are to receive.
~ Meister Eckhart

Dear Father, as I look around every day I see evidence of Your love for me. I see it in the glory of nature, in the eyes of my child, in the helping hands of my parents and the encouraging words of my friends.

I see Your love in the words of Scripture and in the words of songs that play through my mind. You love me. I know it.

Amen.

Seeing Love in the Hard Times

It can be a challenge to remember that God loves you amidst the problems, pain and loss that life brings. It's hard when your heart is breaking and you cry out to God for relief but none seems to come.

Nowhere in Scripture does God promise that life will be easy or pain-free. He does, however, promise to walk beside you through the hard times. He will hold you up when necessary or carry you if that's what you need.

The love of God is most apparent during the painful times of life. However, you may not be able to actually see that until the pain subsides. In looking back you can see where He helped you and how He strengthened you, perhaps even how He surrounded you with loving friends and family.

Your relationship with Him is then strengthened. That may be the "good" of which Romans 8:28 speaks – a closer, more intimate relationship with God.

We know that in all things God works for the good of those who love Him, who have been called according to His purpose.

Romans 8:28

Be strong and courageous. Do not be afraid or terrified because of them, for the LORD your God goes with you; He will never leave you nor forsake you.

Deuteronomy 31:6

The LORD is close to the brokenhearted and saves those who are crushed in spirit.

Psalm 34:18

"No one will be able to stand up against you all the days of your life. As I was with Moses, so I will be with you; I will never leave you nor forsake you."

Joshua 1:5

Cast all your anxiety on Him because He cares for you.

1 Peter 5:7

Consider it pure joy, my brothers, whenever you face trials of many kinds, because you know that the testing of your faith develops perseverance.

James 1:2-3

Praise be to the LORD, for He has heard my cry for mercy. The LORD is my strength and my shield; my heart trusts in Him, and I am helped. My heart leaps for joy and I will give thanks to Him in song.

Psalm 28:6-7

You are a shield around me, O LORD; You bestow glory on me and lift up my head. To the LORD I cry aloud, and He answers me from His holy hill. I lie down and sleep; I wake again, because the LORD sustains me.

Psalm 3:3-5

Maybe the Lord lets some people
get into trouble because that is
the only time they ever think of Him.
~ Anonymous

Dear Father, when I look back at the hard times I've been through, I can see how You helped me make it. I can sense Your love and strength carrying me through the pain.

The memory of those experiences strengthens me every time a new crisis arises. I know that I'm never alone. You will always be there to carry me through the storms of life.

Amen.

Broken Relationships

An old saying states that there's a thin line between love and hate. Both are intense emotions. When you love someone with all your heart, but, for whatever reason (usually many reasons) the relationship is broken, the strong feelings of love may quickly turn to something that is closer to hate, or at least intense dislike. Whatever the reason, it's no fun.

There are of course different kinds of love – friend love, family love, romantic love, love for God, love for Christian brothers and sisters. Love for others is commanded by God so when love turns to negative feelings, there's a problem. The only way to handle the problem is with God's help.

If your love has gone sour, ask Him to fill you with Christian love for that person in your life. He will help you concentrate on his or her good points and remember why you loved him or her in the first place.

Love that flows through you from God is healthy love and demands nothing from you except to be the vessel.

Anyone who claims to be in the light but hates his brother is still in the darkness. Whoever loves his brother lives in the light, and there is nothing in him to make him stumble.

I John 2:9-10

Above all, love each other deeply, because love covers over a multitude of sins.

I Peter 4:8

"By this all men will know that you are My disciples, if you love one another."

John 13:35

The LORD is good to all; He has compassion on all He has made.

Psalm 145:9

Hatred stirs up dissension, but love covers over all wrongs.

Proverbs 10:12

No one has ever seen God; but if we love one another, God lives in us and His love is made complete in us.

I John 4:12

Love is patient, love is kind. It does not envy, it does not boast, it is not proud. It is not rude, it is not self-seeking, it is not easily angered, it keeps no record of wrongs. Love does not delight in evil but rejoices with the truth. It always protects, always trusts, always hopes, always perseveres.

I Corinthians 13:4-7

"You have heard that it was said, 'Love your neighbor and hate your enemy.' But I tell you: Love your enemies and pray for those who persecute you, that you may be sons of your Father in heaven."

Matthew 5:43-45

I have decided to stick with love.
Hate is too great a burden to bear.
~ Martin Luther King, Jr.

Dear Father, hurt is hard to get over. The pain of my broken relationship colors all my feelings toward that person. I can't get past that without Your help. Please show me how to get my thoughts off of myself.

Help me learn to pray for this person – it's not possible to hate someone and pray for them at the same time. So, I choose to go the prayer route. Help me, Father. I can't do it without You.

Amen.

Unconditional Love

Some love relationships are conditional. For example, "I'll love you if you dump your friends and spend all your time with me." Or, "Give up your love for country music ... tennis ... theater ... and like what I like."

It feels like you're always walking on eggshells around a person like this. You never know what will anger him and make you risk losing his "love". This love is conditional on you always pleasing him and doing what he wants.

The only love that is truly unconditional is God's love. He loves you, no matter what. Of course He is disappointed when you disobey Him. He longs for you to return His love. He wants to be important in your life.

He will continually give you more chances to come to Him. He waits for you. He won't turn away. He won't cut you off. He has loved you since before you were born and He will love you always. No matter what.

All the ways of the LORD are loving and faithful for those who keep the demands of His covenant.

Psalm 25:10

"I am with you and will watch over you wherever you go, and I will bring you back to this land. I will not leave you until I have done what I have promised you."

Genesis 28:15

"Here I am! I stand at the door and knock. If any-one hears My voice and opens the door, I will come in and eat with him, and he with Me."

Revelation 3:20

The LORD your God is with you, He is mighty to save. He will take great delight in you, He will quiet you with His love, He will rejoice over you with singing.

Zephaniah 3:17

But when the kindness and love of God our Savior appeared, He saved us, not because of righteous things we had done, but because of His mercy.

Titus 3:4-5

My dear children, I write this to you so that you will not sin. But if anybody does sin, we have one who speaks to the Father in our defense – Jesus Christ, the Righteous One.

1 John 2:1

Search me, O God, and know my heart; test me and know my anxious thoughts. See if there is any offensive way in me, and lead me in the way everlasting.

Psalm 139:23-24

Praise the LORD, O my soul; and forget not all His benefits – who forgives all your sins and heals all your diseases, who redeems your life from the pit and crowns you with love and compassion, who satisfies your desires with good things so that your youth is renewed like the eagle's.

Psalm 103:1-5

God is not proud. He will have us even though we have shown that we prefer everything else to Him.

~ C. S. Lewis

❧

Dear Father, thank You for Your unconditional love. Thank You that I don't have to worry that I'll say the wrong thing or do the wrong thing and cause You to leave me.

Your love is the foundation of my life. Everything else rests on it. Thank You that it is immovable.

Amen.

Love That Binds

There are certain kinds of glue which are advertised to be so strong that they can pick up things like bowling balls. If you happen to glue parts of your body together – fingers for instance – you may need to visit a hospital to get them separated. This is glue that holds tight for a long, long time.

That description of glue could also be a description of love. It binds you to another person so tightly that nothing can come between your hearts. Misunderstandings, differences of opinion, even arguments are worked out, forgiven and forgotten in the light of such love.

God's love for you is even stronger than the strongest human love. It is the "superglue" of all love. You are bound to Him by His love for you. Nothing can ever separate you from His love. You are connected at the heart ... forever.

It is good to praise the Lord and make music to Your name, O Most High, to proclaim Your love in the morning and Your faithfulness at night.

Psalm 92:1-2

"For I know the plans I have for you," declares the Lord, "plans to prosper you and not to harm you, plans to give you hope and a future."

Jeremiah 29:11

In their distress they turned to the Lord, the God of Israel, and sought Him.

2 Chronicles 15:4

O Lord, our Lord, how majestic is Your name in all the earth!

Psalm 8:1

God has said, "Never will I leave you; never will I forsake you." So we say with confidence, "The Lord is my helper; I will not be afraid."

Hebrews 13:5-6

The LORD is a refuge for the oppressed, a stronghold in times of trouble.

Psalm 9:9

Cast your cares on the LORD and He will sustain you; He will never let the righteous fall.

Psalm 55:22

Jesus said to Simon Peter, "Simon son of John, do you truly love Me more than these?" "Yes, Lord," he said, "You know that I love You." Jesus said, "Feed My lambs."

John 21:15

*The purposes of God point
to one simple end – that we should be
as He is, think the same thoughts,
mean the same things,
possess the same blessedness.*

~ George MacDonald

*Dear Father, what a privilege to be bound to
You by love. I am humbled and so unworthy,
yet so grateful and honored. Thank You for
Your love. May others see it in me and feel it
flowing through me.*

Amen.

Loving Your Enemies

You love your family – good for you. You love your friends – that's wonderful. You love the world, that nameless, faceless, global mass of humanity – admirable. How do you feel about your enemies?

You know, the co-worker who stabbed you in the back in order to further her own career. The person who tarnished your reputation in order to make herself look good to others. Yeah, enemies are a lot harder to love. You may even think you're doing okay if you just ignore them instead of striking back at them.

However, God expects a little more from you. Jesus taught that even the pagans, the unbelievers, love their friends. It takes a love that comes from God to love your enemies. Love that goes beyond the boundaries is what sets God's children apart from the world.

It shows that you're different from the average person. Loving your enemies can be the impetus that loves them into God's family. It shows that you belong to God.

"You have heard that it was said, 'Love your neighbor and hate your enemy.' But I tell you: Love your enemies and pray for those who persecute you, that you may be sons of your Father in heaven."

Matthew 5:43-45

The fruit of the Spirit is love, joy, peace, patience, kindness, goodness, faithfulness, gentleness and self-control. Against such things there is no law.

Galatians 5:22-23

He has showed you, O man, what is good. And what does the LORD require of you? To act justly and to love mercy and to walk humbly with your God.

Micah 6:8

If anyone says, "I love God," yet hates his brother, he is a liar. For anyone who does not love his brother, whom he has seen, cannot love God, whom he has not seen.

1 John 4:20

"Do not hate your brother in your heart. Rebuke your neighbor frankly so you will not share in his guilt. Do not seek revenge or bear a grudge against one of your people, but love your neighbor as yourself. I am the Lord."

Leviticus 19:17-18

"In everything, do to others what you would have them do to you, for this sums up the Law and the Prophets."

Matthew 7:12

Love your enemies, do good to them, and lend to them without expecting to get anything back.

Luke 6:35

Do everything without complaining or arguing, so that you may become blameless and pure, children of God without fault in a crooked and depraved generation, in which you shine like stars in the universe as you hold out the word of life.

Philippians 2:14-16

You will find as you look back
upon your life that the moments
when you have really lived,
are the moments when you have
done things in a spirit of love.
                                    ~ Henry Drummond

❧

Dear Father, OK, You're going to have to do
this for me. I can't love my enemies – not in
my own strength. Open my heart, fill it with
love, flow that love through me. Father, may
I be an instrument of Your love to those who
have hurt me most.

Amen.

God Is Number One

There are times in life when your emotional foundations may be completely shaken. One by one the things or situations upon which your world is built or the people you depend on may be taken away.

Perhaps one day you look around and realize that those things which have been your anchors in life are all gone. What do you do?

As difficult as those situations are, they provide the opportunity to experience that God is all you need. There's no doubt that loss of financial security, position, and loss of loved ones are difficult losses to endure. But our God is a jealous God. He wants to be number one in your life. He wants to be more important than any of those things that become your anchor.

His desire isn't based on ego or control. He loves you so much that He desires to be your anchor, your strength and support throughout all of life. His love will do that for you.

"If you love Me, you will obey what I command."

John 14:15

The LORD your God is a consuming fire, a jealous God.

Deuteronomy 4:24

Blessed is the man who does not walk in the counsel of the wicked or stand in the way of sinners or sit in the seat of mockers. But his delight is in the law of the LORD, and on His law he meditates day and night.

Psalm 1:1-2

"No one can serve two masters. Either he will hate the one and love the other, or he will be devoted to the one and despise the other. You cannot serve both God and Money."

Matthew 6:24

We give thanks to You, O God, we give thanks, for Your Name is near; men tell of Your wonderful deeds.

Psalm 75:1

Let the morning bring me word of Your unfailing love, for I have put my trust in You. Show me the way I should go, for to You I lift up my soul.

Psalm 143:8

"Greater love has no one than this, that he lay down his life for his friends."

John 15:13

If anyone obeys His word, God's love is truly made complete in him.

I John 2:5

*God is not greater if you
reverence Him, but you
are greater if you serve Him.*
~ St. Augustine

❧

Dear God, Satan knows where my weaknesses are. He challenges me constantly to push You out of the Number One place in my heart. Help me fight him.

I choose You to be most important in my life. It's a choice I must make many times each day and with Your help and strength, I will always choose You!

Amen.

Love in the Background

Do you enjoy being around a person who continually tries to top everyone else's stories or experiences. You know the type – her illnesses have been the worst, her successes are the greatest, her experiences have been the funniest.

After a while you don't even try to talk to this kind of person because everything you say will be topped, even if the truth is stretched to do so.

What's missing from this person's relationships? Love. There's no love available for others from the type of person who always wants to be the center of attention. Love builds others up. It makes others look good and feel good about themselves. Love makes one person fade to the background and pushes another into the light so her accomplishments will be known and she will feel good about herself.

Love seeks to bring out the best in others and not to brag about oneself. Love isn't about you. Love is about others.

Do nothing out of selfish ambition or vain conceit, but in humility consider others better than yourselves. Each of you should look not only to your own interests, but also to the interests of others.

Philippians 2:3-4

"Therefore, whoever humbles himself like this child is the greatest in the kingdom of heaven."

Matthew 18:4

Two are better than one, because they have a good return for their work: if one falls down, his friend can help him up.

Ecclesiastes 4:9-10

Do not go beyond what is written. Then you will not take pride in one man over against another. For who makes you different from anyone else? What do you have that you did not receive? And if you did receive it, why do you boast as though you did not?

1 Corinthians 4:6-7

Let us consider how we may spur one another on toward love and good deeds.

Hebrews 10:24

Clothe yourselves with humility toward one another, because, "God opposes the proud but gives grace to the humble." Humble yourselves, therefore, under God's mighty hand, that He may lift you up in due time. Cast all your anxiety on Him because He cares for you.

1 Peter 5:5-7

For we are to God the aroma of Christ among those who are being saved and those who are perishing. To the one we are the smell of death; to the other, the fragrance of life.

2 Corinthians 2:15-16

Let us not become conceited, provoking and envying each other.

Galatians 5:26

Treat people as if they were what they ought to be and you help them to become what they are capable of being.
~ *John Wolfgang von Goethe*

Dear Father, it feels so good to be an encouragement to someone else. Help me to know when to stay in the background and let someone else shine. Help me keep my ego in check and know the joy of encouraging someone else into the spotlight.

Amen.

Growing Love

One amazing thing about love is how it grows. When you first come to know God, you think that you couldn't love Him any more than at that moment when your heart first opened to Him.

On the day you marry your sweetheart you feel that the love you share is absolutely the greatest love of all time. The love you feel for the newborn baby you've just birthed is simply beyond measure.

But five years down the road from each of these situations, you can look back and see how immature your honest love was at that point and how it has grown to its present depth. Then you know that your love will continue to grow deeper and stronger all the time.

And when you think you've got no more room in your heart a new child enters the picture, or a new friend, or a deeper understanding of God and His love for you ... and the love in your heart multiplies to share with all. Love is a miracle.

Jesus answered, "I am the way and the truth and the life. No one comes to the Father except through Me."

John 14:6

Physical training is of some value, but godliness has value for all things, holding promise for both the present life and the life to come.

1 Timothy 4:8

"I will instruct you and teach you in the way you should go; I will counsel you and watch over you."

Psalm 32:8

Being confident of this, that He who began a good work in you will carry it on to completion until the day of Christ Jesus.

Philippians 1:6

I pray that you, being rooted and established in love, may have power, together with all the saints, to grasp how wide and long and high and deep is the love of Christ, and to know this love that surpasses knowledge – that you may be filled to the measure of all the fullness of God.

Ephesians 3:17-19

Grow in the grace and knowledge of our Lord and Savior Jesus Christ.

2 Peter 3:18

Build yourselves up in your most holy faith and pray in the Holy Spirit. Keep yourselves in God's love as you wait for the mercy of our Lord Jesus Christ to bring you to eternal life.

Jude 1:20-21

I can do everything through Him who gives me strength.

Philippians 4:13

Love grows by giving. The love we give away is the only love we keep.
~ Elbert Hubbard

Dear Father, love is amazing. It does grow. The more I know Your love, the more I love others. The more people I love, the more my capacity for love grows. It's a miracle. Thank You for starting it all by loving me. Increase my love for You and for others more every day!

Amen.